This Nature Storybook belongs to:

_____

_____

_____

COMMA CATERPILLARS

ORANGE TIP CATERPILLARS

PEACOCK CATERPILLARS

*It's impossible to say exactly when
you'll find caterpillars. It depends on where
you live, and what the weather's like, and all sorts
of other things. The eggs I found were laid in May.
They hatched out into caterpillars in June and changed
their skins four times during the next month or so. The first
three times I didn't see it happen, because they changed
inside their tents. But I did see the fourth time…
The caterpillar on the pea sticks pupated
in the middle of July and became
a butterfly in August.*

For my grandfather, S. H. K., with love
V. F.
For Robert and Chloe
C. V.

First published 1993 by Walker Books Ltd
87 Vauxhall Walk, London SE11 5HJ

This edition published 2015

2 4 6 8 10 9 7 5 3 1

Text © 1993 Vivian French
Illustrations © 1993 Charlotte Voake

This book has been typeset in Calligraphic 810 BT

Printed in China

British Library Cataloguing in Publication Data:
a catalogue record for this book is available from the British Library

ISBN 978-1-4063-6543-6

www.walker.co.uk

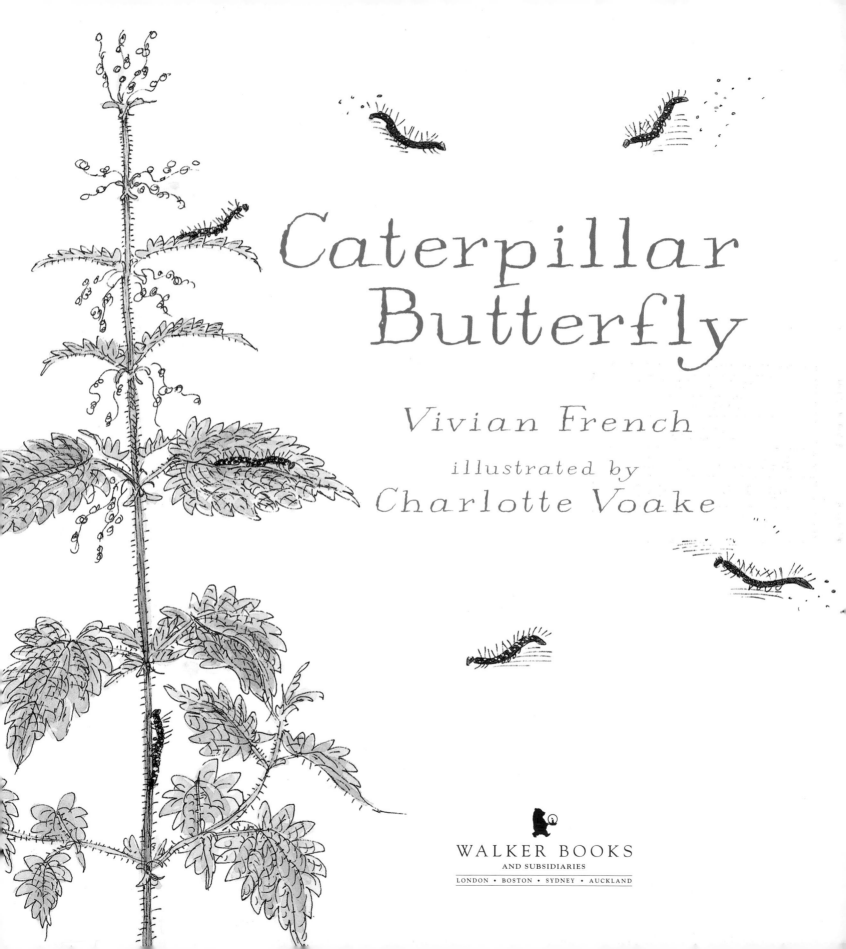

Caterpillar
Butterfly

Vivian French

illustrated by
Charlotte Voake

WALKER BOOKS
AND SUBSIDIARIES
LONDON • BOSTON • SYDNEY • AUCKLAND

My father and my grandfather both liked gardening very much, but my grandfather used to grow stinging nettles. My father didn't; he said they were weeds, and rooted them out.

"Why don't you get rid of your nettles?" I asked my grandfather.

"Stinging nettles grow butterflies," he said. "Go and look."

I went and looked. I couldn't see any butterflies, though. My grandfather turned one of the nettle leaves over to show me the bumps on the back of it, but I didn't know what they were.

"Butterfly eggs," said my grandfather.

"What sort of butterflies?"

My grandfather peered closely at the bumps.

"Haven't got my specs on," he said, "but they could

be Tortoiseshells, or Peacocks. They both like nettles.

If you keep an eye on them you'll see when

the caterpillars hatch out."

"Won't they crawl away?" I asked.

My grandfather straightened up

and looked down at me.

"Humph," he said.

"You just keep watching."

So I did.

NETTLES WILL STING YOU IF YOU TOUCH THEM, BUT THEY WON'T STING THE CATERPILLARS.

THE EGGS ARE DOME-SHAPED, WITH LITTLE RIDGES. EACH EGG IS ABOUT THE SIZE OF THE TOP OF A PIN.

MOST BUTTERFLIES LAY THEIR EGGS IN ONES AND TWOS, MOVING FROM PLANT TO PLANT. PEACOCK AND TORTOISESHELL BUTTERFLIES LAY LOTS OF EGGS AT ONCE.

9

Nothing happened at all for two days. It rained very hard on the second day, but the eggs were quite safe.

The next day there were lots and lots
of little tiny caterpillars crawling on the
nettle leaves. The eggs were papery
and empty. I squashed some
with my fingernail.

THE CATERPILLARS EAT
THEIR WAY OUT OF THE
EGGS WHEN THEY'RE
READY TO HATCH,
AND STAY TOGETHER
IN A BIG CROWD.

THEY MAKE A WEB OF
WHITE SILK BETWEEN
THE STEM OF THE PLANT
AND THE LEAVES.
IT'S LIKE A TENT.

WHEN THEY'VE EATEN
ALL THE LEAVES NEARBY,
THEY MOVE ON AND
MAKE A NEW TENT.

My grandfather came over to see

what I was doing.

"Ah," he said, "Peacock caterpillars."

"Do they eat cabbage?" I asked.

I'd seen caterpillars on cabbages.

He shook his head. "Caterpillars are fussy eaters. If you put a nettle-eating caterpillar on a cabbage it'll set off to look for nettles, and if it can't find any it'll sit down and die rather than eat cabbage."

SOME OF THE CATERPILLARS YOU SEE ON CABBAGES ARE

ORANGE TIP CATERPILLARS EAT LADY'S SMOCK AND GARLIC MUSTARD. (SOMETIMES THEY EAT EACH OTHER.)

14

COMMA
CATERPILLARS
LIKE HOPS BEST,
BUT SOMETIMES
THEY HAVE
TO MAKE
DO WITH
NETTLES.

CABBAGE WHITES. THEY LOVE CABBAGE.

PEACOCK,
SMALL TORTOISESHELL,
AND RED ADMIRAL
CATERPILLARS ALL
LIKE NETTLES BEST.

15

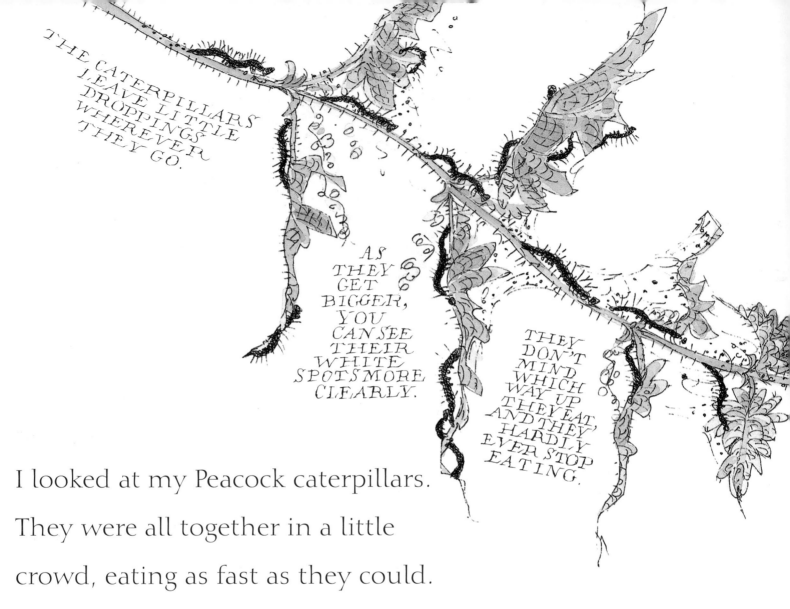

THE CATERPILLARS LEAVE LITTLE DROPPINGS WHEREVER THEY GO.

AS THEY GET BIGGER, YOU CAN SEE THEIR WHITE SPOTS MORE CLEARLY.

THEY DON'T MIND WHICH WAY UP THEY EAT, AND THEY HARDLY EVER STOP EATING.

I looked at my Peacock caterpillars.

They were all together in a little

crowd, eating as fast as they could.

"Won't the birds eat them?" I asked.

"Couldn't we cover them up?"

"No need," said my grandfather.

"Caterpillars that don't hide away are really saying,

'I'm poisonous – keep off!' And the birds know that."

16

He pulled his pipe out of his pocket and very,
very gently nudged one of the caterpillars.

It curled itself up at once and fell off the leaf.

"There," he said. "Even if something does come along
looking for a snack, the caterpillar might still escape."

"Can I make one curl up?" I stuck my finger out.

"Don't touch them," my grandfather said.

"Some spiny caterpillars can give you a rash,
and other kinds leave a nasty smell on
your fingers. Besides, you might hurt them."

THEY HAVE VELVETY BODIES AND SHINY HEADS.
LOOK AT THEIR SPINY BACKS!
THEY HAVE THREE PAIRS OF LEGS
IN FRONT, WITH LITTLE
CLAWS ON THEM, AND
STUMPIER LEGS
FURTHER DOWN.

I went on watching the caterpillars.

They were getting bigger. By the second Saturday in July they had eaten nearly all the plant they had hatched out on and were crawling over the other nettles.

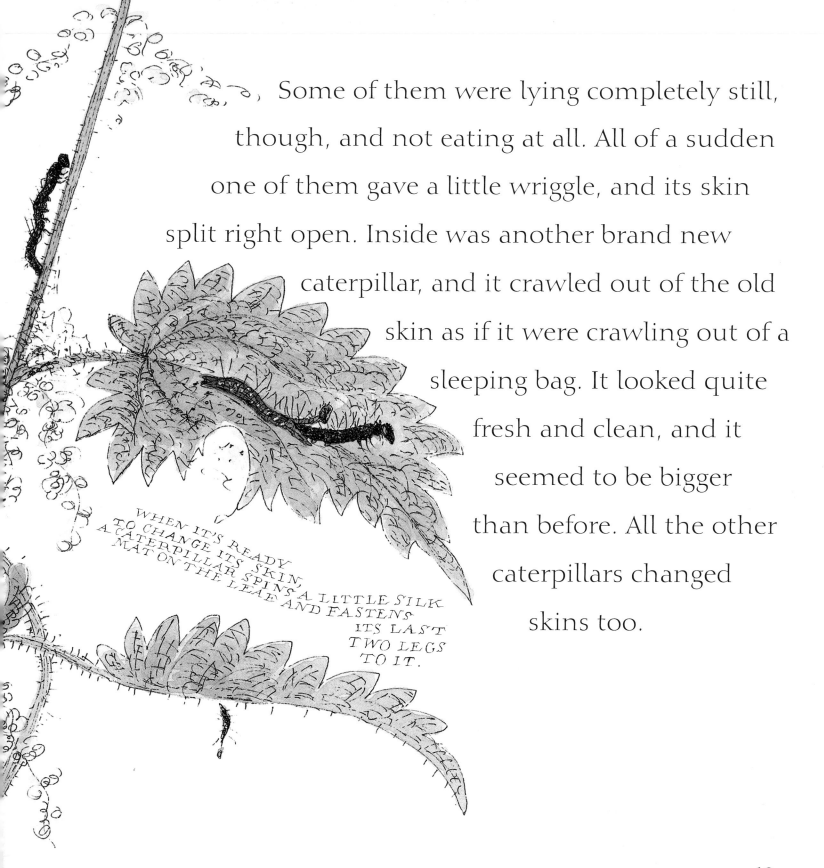

Some of them were lying completely still, though, and not eating at all. All of a sudden one of them gave a little wriggle, and its skin split right open. Inside was another brand new caterpillar, and it crawled out of the old skin as if it were crawling out of a sleeping bag. It looked quite fresh and clean, and it seemed to be bigger than before. All the other caterpillars changed skins too.

WHEN IT'S READY
TO CHANGE ITS SKIN,
A CATERPILLAR SPINS A LITTLE SILK
MAT ON THE LEAF AND FASTENS
ITS LAST
TWO LEGS
TO IT.

My grandfather said that was just what it was,
but the proper name for it was a pupa.

"But where's the caterpillar gone?" I asked.
All the bits of caterpillar were inside the case,
he said, and they were changing.

WHEN THEY'RE READY TO
PUPATE, THE
CATERPILLARS
LEAVE THEIR
NETTLES.

EACH ONE OF THEM
FINDS A
PLACE TO
BE ON ITS
OWN.

IT MIGHT BE UP A
TREE, A FENCE,
A STICK, OR A TWIG.

22

EACH
CATERPILLAR
MAKES
A TINY WHITE
PAD...

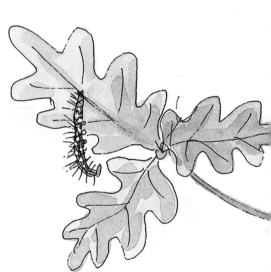

THEN
ATTACHES ITS
BACK LEGS TO
IT, AND HANGS
UPSIDE DOWN.

SOON THEIR SKIN PEELS
OFF, LEAVING BEHIND
A BEAUTIFUL PUPA.
IT'S GREEN IF IT'S ON
A LEAF AND BROWN
IF IT'S ON A
TWIG.

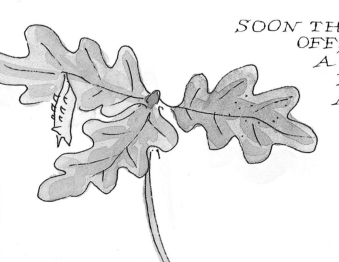

Just this once, I was allowed to bring the stick with the little case on it into the kitchen. I watched for ten whole days and on the tenth day the pupa went very, very dark.

The next morning I was eating my breakfast when my grandfather suddenly said, "LOOK!"

I rushed to see, and the case of the pupa

had split. Something was crawling out …

but it didn't look a bit like a butterfly.

It was crumpled, and it looked damp,

and it wasn't at all a pretty colour.

"It must have gone wrong,"
I said, feeling very sad.

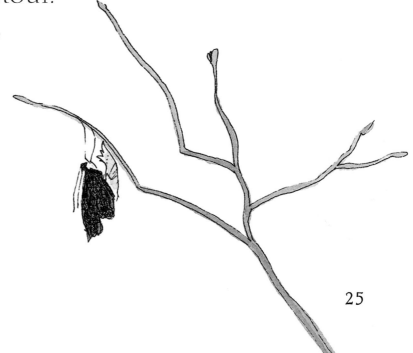

Very gently, my grandfather

lifted the stick and put it on

the window-ledge in the sunshine.

The creature crawled slowly up

the stick, and stopped.

Little by little it began to stretch out.

It was just like watching a flower

unfolding itself, only it had

wings instead of petals.

THE WINGS
OF THE
BUTTERFLY
UNFOLD AS LIQUID
IS PUMPED INTO
ITS VEINS.

THE WINGS HAVE
TO DRY FOR AN
HOUR OR TWO
BEFORE IT
CAN FLY.

26

And the wings began to tremble, and to shine in the sunlight, and then suddenly there it was – a real butterfly, with spidery legs and its wings spread wide open.

It was so lovely that I couldn't say anything at all. Then its wings fluttered and it flew off into the garden – the very newest butterfly there.

COMMA

PEACOCK

RED ADMIRAL

COMMA

Index

Look up the pages to find out about
all these caterpillar and butterfly things.
Don't forget to look at both kinds of words:
this kind and *THIS KIND*.

LARGE WHITE

ORANGE TIP

ORANGE TIP

COMMON BLUE

COMMON BLUE
CATERPILLAR

Note to Parents

Sharing books with children is one of the best ways to help them learn. And it's one of the best ways they learn to read, too.

Nature Storybooks are beautifully illustrated, award-winning information picture books whose focus on animals has a strong appeal for children. They can be read as stories, revisited and enjoyed again and again, inviting children to become excited about a subject, to think and discover, and to want to find out more.

Each book is an adventure into the real world that broadens children's experience and develops their curiosity and understanding – and that's the best kind of learning there is.

Note to Teachers

Nature Storybooks provide memorable reading experiences for children in Key Stages 1 and 2 (Years 1–4), and also offer many learning opportunities for exploring a topic through words and pictures.

By working with the stories, either individually or together, children can respond to the animal world through a variety of activities, including drawing and painting, role play, talking and writing.

The books provide a rich starting-point for further research and for developing children's knowledge of information genres.

Nature Storybooks support the literacy curriculum in a variety of ways, providing:

- a focus for a whole class topic
- high-quality texts for guided reading
- a resource for the class read-aloud programme
- information texts for the class and school library for developing children's individual reading interests

Find more information on how to use Nature Storybooks in the classroom at
www.walker.co.uk/naturestorybooks

Nature Storybooks support KS 1–2 English and KS 1–2 Science